HELP!!!

I'm in Middle School...

How Will I Survive?

A lighthearted approach to a serious subject

Merry L. Gumm

This book is dedicated to
my husband, Dennis;
my children, Amy and Laurie;
& my grandchildren, Mason and Kaylee.

First Printing October 2004
© Copyright 2004 by Merry L. Gumm
NSR Publications Douglass, KS

Library of Congress Control Number: 2004113498
ISBN 0-9761724-5-3

CONTENTS

I Just Can't Get Good Grades...

What Should I Do?

☺ THINGS THAT WORK

☞ **Write Down Everything.**
Write, write, write, write, write. I can't say it
enough times. And the more detail the better.
If you don't know when there is a test, you
won't study for it. If you
don't know an assignment is
due, you won't have it there
on time. I hope you are
already writing things down.
If not, start now making it a
habit – something you do
every day.

☞ **No Zeros**.
Make this your number one goal. Not handing
in an assignment and taking a zero on it will
kill a grade faster than water running off a wart
hog. If you haven't finished an assignment,
either hand in what part of it you have done or
(if your teacher allows it) finish it at home
tonight and hand it in tomorrow. It will be late,
and you will lose points. But, hey, it's not a big,
fat, ugly zero. Just don't hand in nothing –
hand in something.

☞ **Complete all your assignments exactly as the teacher has asked.**

Once you have finished an assignment, YOU BE THE TEACHER. Grade the assignment like the teacher would. *Reread the directions* and make sure you have included every detail the teacher has asked for. If you don't do something the teacher has asked for, you will lose points. If you forget to do enough things the teacher has asked for, your grade will be in the toilet. So, you be the teacher. Be tough on yourself. If something is missing, add it. If you didn't do a good job on something, redo it. Your study buddy (we'll talk about this later) could help you here, too. Exchange papers and be the teacher for each other. Be tough!!!! Help each other out – together you can both reach for that "A". At the very least, your grade will improve.

☞ **Listen to the teachers.**

I know, I know, it is easy to tune them out. You think you could probably get the information from your friend later. Besides, thinking about the game today is much more interesting. The trouble with tuning out  the teachers is that they are telling you something that you need to hear – some last minute instructions, answering questions about the assignment, giving you a hint about the assignment to make it a bit easier, telling you about an upcoming test, or whatever. Most teachers don't talk that long anyway, so focus, look at them, and listen to what they have to say. If you tend to forget things, jot down a few notes to help you remember some of the important things.

But this is sooooo boring, can't I just doodle while I'm listening? Not really a good idea. Try your hardest to ...

☞ **Look at the teacher while he is talking.**
Oh, I know you can listen when you are looking down or doodling (I do it, too). But, if you're not looking at the teacher, it's easy to start daydreaming of other things. And before you know it, you have missed some things the teacher has said. Or maybe you have totally

zoned out and have no idea what the teacher is talking about now.

But sometimes I look at the teacher and still wander off and daydream. Daydreaming **is** easy to do. But if you are looking at the teacher, you will be less likely to daydream. Even if you are daydreaming, unless you have that deer-in-the-headlights look, the teacher won't know. So, if for no other reason, look at him -- fake him out.

☞ **Go to school every day.**
Unless you are sick or just can't make it for a really, really important reason, make yourself go to school every day. Even missing one day can get you behind in your work -- the teacher just keeps assigning things whether you're there are not. The more days you miss, the harder it is to catch up, to get everything done. And then, you miss what the teacher says, too. If you don't understand what you're doing, it is even harder to do the missing assignment. It can begin to be so overwhelming that you just want to give up. Make it easy on yourself; go to school every day. Your friends are there anyway.

I stayed up late last night. I'm tired. Oh, please, missing one day of school won't hurt that much, will it? Don't do it; don't let that temptation get to you. If you miss this day, it will be easier to make an excuse again and pretty soon you will be right back where you started. Come on, you can do it. Make yourself get up and go – every day.

☞ **Be on time to school.**
This is kind of like going to school every day. Oh sure, you are there every day, but those minutes you are missing at the beginning of each day add up. You will miss what the teacher says at the beginning of that day and, as we know, that isn't good. If you are in a school with different classes each period, you are missing part or all of that same class every day. Think of it as getting a zero (a big ugly 0) for attendance in that class. Being on time to school is as important as being there every day.

All right, all right. I'll get up. I'm beginning to see that getting to school on time every day is important.

☞ **Get a good night's sleep.**
We already know missing or being late for school isn't helping. But, if you're sleepy, your body may be at school, but your head won't be. Sleeping at school with your eyes open or shut is almost as bad as staying at home. So, give your body and brain a break. Give them plenty of rest so they will be ready to do their best work at school.

☹ THINGS THAT WON'T WORK

☞ Trying to remember everything.
To make this work, you'd have to be an elephant – they don't forget anything – or do they?

☞ Trying to get by with a smile.
You do have a nice smile, but it isn't going to get you a good grade. Being friendly with the teacher and smiling a lot might have worked in elementary school, but, alas, you are almost an adult now. And that smile that used to work so well for you just isn't going to work for you now.

☞ Getting someone else to do your work for you.
This just isn't going to work for you in the long term either. Your friends have their own work to do – if you wait for them to do your work, you're probably going to be waiting a looooooong time. And, if you are depending on the Internet to find something to hand in, that's not really a good idea either. Teachers are getting wiser and wiser – there is even software now to tell if a paper has come from an Internet source. So, don't risk getting busted big time, just buckle down and do the paper yourself.

I Don't Know When Assignments and Tests Are Due...

What Should I Do?

The math test is Tuesday. That social studies project is due Thursday, and the English test is Friday. Wait a minute. I think the English test is Tuesday and the Math test is Friday. My brain is starting to melt down.

☺ THINGS THAT WORK

☞ **Write down what you have to do every day, every class period!**

That way you won't be surprised. You will know when assignments are due, when there is a test, and other important dates. Keep some kind of a daily planner to write all your assignments in – everything you have to do. Different people write down things in different ways, so be creative about what works for you.

Wow! This writing everything down really works.

Here are some ideas that work. Keep trying until you find one that works for you.

🖉 An agenda.

This will have sections for each class period of the day. Write in it EVERY class period, EVERY day. Write what assignments you have and when they are due. Write when the dance is. Write when you have a test. Write, write, write. Write everything.

But it's kind of big to carry with me all the time. Anyway, I keep losing it in my locker.

🖉 A daily plan book.

This will have pages for each day of the week. If you are having trouble with the agenda (and its size), try buying a plan book that will fit in your pocket or your backpack or your purse. That way you won't be leaving it places, and it won't get lost in your locker. Wherever you decide to keep it, keep it handy where it's easy to get to. If you have to dig for it, you probably won't use it. Again, write in it every day, every hour. Write down absolutely everything (plans you made with your friends for tomorrow, to study for your test Tuesday) – even things that you think you can remember. You won't remember, trust me!

The planner is too small. I can't seem to keep track of it.

✏ **A page in the front of your binder**.
If you are having trouble keeping track of something separate, try keeping track of assignments and other things right in the binder where you keep your homework. If you have a binder for each class, keep the assignments, notes, and other reminders for that class in the front of the binder. *This is great. Nothing extra to worry about.*

Woops. I spoke too soon. The holes ripped, and the page fell out of my binder. Hole reinforcements will save you here. But don't wait until the page falls out; put the reinforcements on the paper the first day.

✏ **Your hand, your arm, whatever you can't lose**.
Some may think you're crazy, but it does work. Some of us just have trouble keeping track of things. Write what you absolutely have to know for the next day on your hand (or arm if there isn't enough

room on your hand). You can't lose it, and you will know what you need for the next day: what assignments you have, and what is due. If there is something that you need to know several days away, ask your parents to help you remember. They can put it on a calendar or on a plan book that is kept at home – it's harder to lose when you're not carrying it around all the time.

I look like the tattooed circus performer, but at least I know what is going on tomorrow.

☞ **Find a Study Buddy.**

Even if you try your hardest, sometimes you will forget to write something down (or you can't read what you wrote). This is where a study buddy will help. You can either call each other on a regular basis to check to be sure you got everything down right and to study for tests, or you can just call each other when you have a question. Your choice. But, the important thing is that you have someone to call if you need some help or just moral support.

☞ **Use the School.**

Most schools have a way for you to find out what the basic assignment is. You might not get details, but at least you can get some general information. An example would be a "homework hotline". Teachers keep this updated daily so if you get home and can't remember what you did in class, this will help jog your memory.

☹ **THINGS THAT WON'T WORK**

☞ **Trying to remember everything.**

You're young. You'd think you should be able to remember what happened today. But, with everyone telling you everything – teachers, parents, friends, enemies – it just isn't possible. So, just give up and figure out a way to write it down.

Yikes. There's a test today.

☞ **Calling your teacher.**

This might   seem like a good idea. She would have all the information, and who better to get the straight scoop from than your teacher. BUT, can you imagine how many calls she would get if you ALL called her? So, listen in class.   If you forgot to write it down and just can't remember, call a friend instead.

Your teacher probably DOES have a life and won't be home anyway.

I Keep Losing
My Assignments...

What Should I Do?

☺ THINGS THAT WORK

What is important here is to get organized. If
you get everything organized, you will be less
likely to lose assignments – or anything else for
that matter. You can use one of the ideas I give
you here, or you can use something else. But
do something so that you know where things
are when you need them. Pick something that
works for YOU. Try one you think you like. If
that doesn't work, then try another. Keep
trying until you find one that works.

*How about this one. Only one binder? This
one sounds just right for me.*

☞ **Use one binder and keep everything in it.**
Sometimes keeping everything in one place
helps because you only have one place to look
for whatever you need. One clue, though, be
sure to clip everything in it. If you cram papers
into it, they are going to fall out and you will be
no better off than you were before.

*Well, I thought this would work. But when I
get in a hurry I stuff my papers in it. Now it*

is so full, it will explode when I open it.
Maybe breaking it down a little would help.

☞ **Use a binder for each class or subject.**
Sometimes this is better than one binder because having a binder for each class naturally organizes assignments. If you have your social studies binder with you, for instance, then you should have everything you need for social studies that day. A big part of this is making sure that  you keep absolutely everything you need for a certain class in the right binder and that you have the right binder when you get to class. If you start sticking things from math in your science binder, for example, then you can kiss this system goodbye.

Now that I think about it, this one might not be for me either. I would still probably stuff things in it, and although it would be better than one binder, I think I would like to try something where I didn't have to clip papers.

☞ **Use a pocket folder for assignments**.
Label the left side "unfinished assignments" and the right side "finished assignments". Put assignments in the left side of the pocket folder that need to be started or you still need to work

on them. If you work on the assignment but don't finish it, put it back in the left side of the folder. When you finish an assignment, put it in the right side of the folder. When you leave school for the day, check the left side "unfinished assignments" to see what books you need to take home to complete assignments. When everything is on the right side of the folder, then you know you are done for the evening. (Helpful hint: Put the due date on the assignment instructions. Then you will know when it has to be on the right side of the folder under "finished assignments".)

☞ **Clean your locker.**
I'll bet you have finished (or almost finished) assignments in there that need to be turned in. Your locker is probably already cleaner now that you're using binders or a pocket folder to organize (you won't have all those stray papers floating around), but in the best of systems some things get away from us. Keep your locker as clean and organized as possible – or at least clean it regularly (once every week or two). Then it won't get to be such a monstrous mess. Applying this to your room at home would probably put a smile on your mom's face, too. And you might even find something you thought was lost long ago.

I Can't Get Everything Done...

What Should I Do?

☺ THINGS THAT WORK

☞ Stay focused at school.
You have to be there anyway. It's going to be a long day (and a long year) if you sit and stare off into space. The day will go much faster if you keep yourself busy. So, as long as you have to be at school, keep busy doing your schoolwork every minute you are there. The minutes are valuable – don't waste even one of them. Do yourself a favor – make the day go faster and get something done that is going to have to be done anyway. Besides, if you get your work done at school (or the bus ride home), then you can **do** whatever you're daydreaming about when you get home.

☞ Set a study time at home to finish the work you didn't get done at school!
The staying busy part will probably help you get most of your work finished. But, sometimes you need some time outside of school to finish. Tell yourself that you are going to set a certain time each evening to finish your daily work, study for a test, or whatever you need to do for the next day. For

some people, that might be right after school so you can get everything finished and then have the rest of the evening to do whatever it is that YOU want to do. Some people need a down time (a time to relax, play, chill out) between school and study time to be able to concentrate again. Whichever is best for you doesn't matter. But, as Nike says, JUST DO IT!

☞ **Do the assignment you dislike the most, FIRST.**

At least sometimes, for homework do the assignment that you dislike the most, first (and we all have that class that we just hate to go to – mine was social studies). If you always do the assignments for the classes you like first saving the ones you don't like for last, it is easy to be "too tired" to do that last assignment – because you dread it so much. Sooo, do the dreaded one first because you probably won't skip out on the assignments for the classes you like.

☞ **Go to after school tutoring.**

If your school has a tutor time after school, go there. You get quiet time to study (many times in a library so there are books you can use for projects or other things), and there are usually teachers there to help if you get stuck.

Ugh! That sounds like more school. It may seem like it, but this time you're in control. You decide what to do and in what order. But there is a teacher if you WANT help and other books if you need them. Just think. You could be done with your homework BEFORE you leave school. And nothing but free time at home. *What a relief.*

☹ THINGS THAT WON'T WORK

☞ **Procrastinating**.
This is a big word that means "putting off until tomorrow what you can do today." If a teacher gives you an assignment that is due in 3 days, a week, or whatever, begin the assignment that day or evening. Do a little each day. If you wait until the day it is due before you start on it, you probably aren't going to get it done. And if you do finish it, you probably won't do a very good job on it. Don't be a bump on a log. Get in there and get started.

My Friends Are Saying Mean Things About Me . . .

What Should I Do?

☺ THINGS THAT WORK

☞ Look at yourself – on the inside.

The mirror won't do any good here; you have to really soul search. Ask yourself why people are saying these things. Are you doing something that would cause it?

No. I don't think I'm doing anything. I really have no idea, though.

You might have to ask someone who is still being nice to you to find the answer. (Parents can be a help here. They know you better than anyone.) Maybe you are doing something without knowing it to cause friends treat you like this. We can't see ourselves like others see us. Sometimes things come off differently than we intended – we offend someone and don't know it; we say something in a *"tone"* that gives off negative vibes. Someone else might be able to give us an answer. *Be prepared for the answer, though.* That answer can be hard to swallow, but in the end it will be worth it.

☞ **Ask yourself some questions.**
Now that you have asked someone else questions, ask yourself some questions.

? Would "friends" say mean things about me? Are they really my friends? I don't know about you, but with friends like this, enemies might be better to hang out with.

Friend or enemy? Hummm.

? Am I wasting my time trying to be friends with people who don't like me? It's harsh, but sometimes people we like don't always like us back. Maybe this is the case here. Step back a little and look around; there are probably some really nice people out there who would enjoy your company.

? Why do I want to be friends with these people? Again, some real soul searching will help here. Be honest with yourself. You might decide that they aren't your type anyway.

? Am I doing it because they have something I don't have – like popularity or an older brother with a car? The popular people always look like they are having so much fun. But, if this is the main reason you are hanging with them, then it probably won't last anyway. Friends usually have things in common they like to do together.

? *Could I use my time more wisely by approaching people who do NOT say mean things about me?* Now you are on the right track. Find those people who want to be around you and will tell others all the good things about you rather than the negative things. You're a great person. Actually, if you look close enough, you might find someone who has been hanging around you wanting to be **your** friend, but you have been kind of ignoring them. Give this – or another – new person a chance. They may turn out to be the friend of a lifetime.

Now that you have had a heart to heart talk with yourself and others, you hopefully have at least some of the answers you were looking for. You're ready. Put these answers into action. It may be that you want to look around for new friends or just hang around with fewer people – the ones who are nice to you and value your friendship. There is that old saying, "You don't really know who your friends are until you need them." Your real friends will stick with you no matter what. The others weren't really your friends anyway. Besides, some people are just not very nice.

☹ THINGS THAT WON'T WORK

☞ Getting mad.

It helps you get things off your chest, but getting mad won't REALLY help. A better way to get things off your chest is to talk with someone – a friend, parents, brother or sister, teacher. (As a last resort you could go to a place away from everyone and let out a big SCREEEEEAM.) When you get mad, it's easy to do things you regret later. And it won't really help the situation. If you do things when you are mad, you may be in more trouble now than you were before you got mad.

☞ Holding grudges.

You could make yourself sick (really) doing this. Your focus will be on negative things that will draaagggg you down. Get rid of the negative; surround yourself with people who want to be around you and say nice things about you. Get out there and have fun with life.

☞ Believing what is being said about you.

Just because they say it doesn't mean it's true. For whatever reason, sometimes people say things that are totally, totally not true. Think about what is good about you, about your life, and forget about what was said – it's not true anyway.

I Don't Have Any Friends . . .

What Should I Do?

☺ THINGS THAT WORK

☞ **"If you like yourself, you'll have good company 24 hours a day."**
"You are the best friend that you will ever have."
No kidding. So, be everything you want a friend to be – pamper yourself, say nice things to yourself, do nice things for yourself. Treat yourself like royalty. Now that you have at least one friend (*yourself, remember*), let's get started finding some others.

☞ **"To have friends, you have to BE one."**
Oh, so true. Sometimes you can actually try too hard to find friends. If you will just be your wonderful self being nice to people, helping when they need help, talking to them whenever you find that "hi" opportunity, and so on, people that want to hang around you will begin to appear. Wow! Friends. Continue being your wonderful self -- they will stick around.

Sometimes I'm not sure how to be a good friend. I haven't had much practice you know.

Sometimes it IS hard to know what makes a good friend. Try some of these on for size:

✎ **Smile at people.**
Smiling, and laughing for that matter, are infectious. It doesn't have to be a big, teethy smile – that probably will look fake anyway. Just a nice turn-the-corners-of-your-mouth-a-little-upward smile. And if you can squeak out a little "hi" while you're at it, that would help, also.

A *little* much but who could resist a person this happy.

✦ Have a pleasant expression on your face.

Oh, I know you can't be happy all the time; everyone is sad or angry sometimes. But people like to hang with others who are usually in a good mood. Your face shows your mood. So put that pleasant expression on your face (even if you are not in a good mood). You don't have to be smiling, but you don't want to look like the Grinch either. Who knows, if you concentrate on at least having a pleasant look on your face, your mood may improve.

✦ Give compliments to others.

You have to be careful with this one. Give compliments that are deserved – and be careful not to go overboard. Some kids give compliments when they don't mean it, and others will catch on quickly to that. Say something nice that you REALLY mean, and spit it out – with that pleasant expression on your face, of course. Friends are truthful with each other. If someone deserves a compliment, give it. But be sincere.

✦ Be a good listener.

People like to talk about themselves. Talking is the easy part. Being a good listener is really important, and that's hard sometimes. Think of it. Everyone is talking and no one is listening!  Is that confusing or what. So, **zip that lip** and listen to others. You will be a hit.

✋ Be kind to others.

Do nice things for other people. One way to be nice is to offer to help others – like with their homework, carrying things, or picking up things that have been dropped. If you see someone who has dropped absolutely everything in the hall (books, papers, and pencils everywhere – *how embarrassing*), stop and help them pick it up – even if you are late for class. The teacher will probably understand. If she doesn't, you will have probably made a friend. Being kind to others is actually giving some of yourself to them, and they will appreciate that.

✋ Show a REAL interest in what others do.

This goes along with being a good listener. If you show a real interest in what others are doing, you will naturally be listening to them because you are truly interested. Even more, take an ACTIVE interest in what others are doing. Give it a try. It might be fun and you will have found a new hobby and someone to share that hobby with.

✋ Be willing to share.

A sharing person is a nice person to hang around. And this doesn't just mean sharing things. Sharing things is a good way to get started. But good friends will also share thoughts. If you are sad and need someone to talk with, sharing your sadness can somehow make you less sad. If you are afraid or worried or whatever, friends can help each other by sharing thoughts with each other.

✂ Be open and friendly with people.
This isn't always easy. Sometimes the people you are nice to aren't nice back. If you ask someone if they had a nice weekend, (with that pleasant expression on your face, of course) then it gives them the chance to say something back. Most will answer back nicely. Then you can try to continue the conversation. If they aren't nice back, then walk away. That is not the type of friend that you want anyway.

You might have to take a hit or two to your old self esteem, but if you dust yourself off, get back up, and try again, it will be worth it in the end. There are some really nice people out there. Now go out and find them.

☞ Introduce yourself to people – let them get to know you.
I know this is a really hard one, especially if you're shy (like I am). Sometimes you want to talk to them, but when you go up, the words just don't want to come out. Your mouth just won't spit out the words. Or your brain shuts down and you can't think of anything to say. (Been there, done that.) This is where having a hobby and common interests will help. It will be easier if you will look for "hi" opportunities,

like when you are assigned to the same project in science (you have to sit together anyway, so introduce yourself) or you are both asked to be on the track relay team (if you have to run together on the same team, it would be nice to know who your teammates are). If you keep your eyes out for these "hi" opportunities, introducing yourself will be easier. It's like bungee jumping. It gets scarier the longer you stand up there and think about it – so just go. And, one more thing, like riding a bike or anything else, the more you do something, the easier it is. That goes for introducing yourself, too. It doesn't seem like it now, but it WILL get easier the more you do it.

I don't know if I can do that. Don't think about it. Walk up and say, *"Hey, what's up?"* At least then the other person has to say something and you're home free.

☞ **Ask someone to sit or walk with them or to join in what they are doing.**

Like the introducing, this is hard at first. Your knees might be shaking; your face getting red. (*That's me, I was always a blusher. I thought sometimes I wouldn't survive, but look at me now. I made it.*) You're ready: take a deep breath, get every ounce of courage that you have, and JUST DO IT (*Thanks* NIKE). Again, look for "hi" opportunities, and it won't seem so awkward. A word of caution here. You want to be sure to "ask" to join in – not demand. You don't want to come off too strong.

☞ Join a club or sports team.

Think of what interests you the most and find a club or team (which is really just a group of people hanging around together doing the same thing at the same time). You'll be happy doing what you like to do and pretty soon you will be sharing it with others.  People will start talking with you and, before you even realize it, I'll bet you will have at least one friend and probably more.

☞ Find a hobby.

This is kind of like the club thing, but you don't have to join anything for this one if you don't want to. Find something you enjoy, like reading, doing puzzles, collecting baseball cards or penguins, or playing games. Now, you have something to talk to other people about when you're hanging out.

Is sleeping a hobby?

☞ Invite them to your house.

Eventually you will want to go one step further and invite someone to your house. If you feel closer to just one person, invite that person over. Have something planned to do that you know interests both of you. You don't want it to be a big production; it could just be eating pizza and playing computer games. Do something that you know that you and the hopefully-friend-after-this will have fun doing.

If you feel awkward with just one person, invite several people from the club or team over. Make sure you have something planned that they will want to do. Beware though: Be flexible. A plan is great. But if something else more fun shows up, don't be afraid to do that instead.

☞ **Hang around places where people are.**
People like to be with other people, so they hang out together. Look around. There are usually several popular places where kids go after school. It might be a recreation center. Or it might be a park a few blocks from school. You might have to follow some kids after school (discretely, of course – you don't want them to know you are following them) to see where they go. You might have to do this several times with different groups of kids. Once you know where the kids are hanging out, pick one that you enjoy and hang out there too. Then you can put some of the other things that work into practice -- like introducing yourself.

☹ **THINGS THAT WON'T WORK**

☞ **Keeping to yourself and not talking to anyone.**
Not only will this not work, but it is so boring. You do have at least that one friend (*yourself,*

remember), so be nice to yourself and find another friend for you both to hang out with.

I just don't know if I can do it. I am soooooooo shy. What if they ignore me or something. They might, but they're ignoring you now, right (but then you haven't even let them know you might want to be their friend). And they might be just as shy as you are thinking the same things that you are. One of you is going to have to do the NIKE thing and JUST DO IT. So if for nothing else, do it for their sake. They might just think *you* are ignoring *them.*

☞ **Believing that no one could like you.**
Hey, you already have a whole slew of people that like you already. That one friend (*yourself, okay).* Your parents, your brother, sister, your grandparents, your teacher. The list is endless.

I love these people to death, but, hey, I can't hang out with them all the time. I need someone my own age. Here is where you go back to the THINGS THAT WORK section. *Like yourself. Be a friend.* Go out there and find someone else who wants a friend. There are others feeling just like you. Sometimes you have to work at it to find them.

☞ **Doing things that would turn people off.** These are sure-fire things that would send people running the other way. Doing them would make it extremely difficult to find and keep a friend. Besides, some people run really fast which would make it hard to catch them. The trick is this: Don't do things to start them running.

Definite NO-NO'S.

💣* *Being bossy.* It would be nice, but you can't have your way all the time. Others have good ideas, too. Listen to them; theirs might even be better than yours.

💣* *Telling others what to do and how to do it.* This goes along with being bossy. They have minds of their own and without exercise, their minds will just wither and go away. You wouldn't want to be responsible for that would you. So, let others decide what they want to do and how to do it. You stick with deciding what YOU are going to do. I don't know about you, but it's a tough job for me to take care of myself. I wouldn't want the responsibility of taking care of someone else anyway.

♦* *Telling others constantly they are doing things wrong.* There is a fine line here. If someone is truly doing something harmful to themselves or others, you might want to consider stepping in and, in a nice way, telling them. But your thoughts are only YOUR opinions. They may not agree that they are doing anything wrong. Besides, there is usually more than one way to do something. They may just be doing it another way. And no one wants to be told all the time they are doing things wrong. So, unless it is really serious, button your lip – or zip it or whatever. Mum is the word.

♦* *Talking about yourself all the time.* This falls smack dab in the middle of being a good listener. In a conversation, there are two or more people (unless you are talking to yourself and that is what we are trying to get away from here). Each person in the conversation should have the same amount of talk time. Tell yourself that you are going to listen as much as you are going to talk.

♦* *Being mean.* Oooh. No one wants to be around a mean person for very long. And you certainly don't want a mean person for a friend. Have you ever heard the old saying, "With a friend like you, I don't need enemies."

I don't think I'm mean. How do I know if others see me as mean? Follow the Golden Rule: **Do unto others as you would have others do unto you.** So, don't to anything to someone else that you would not want them doing to you. It's that simple.

💣* *Talking about other students behind their backs.* No one likes to be talked about. The quickest way to send people running is to find out that you have said unkind things about them. Make it a rule: Don't say anything about someone that you wouldn't say to their face.

💣* *Being negative and sarcastic.* People like to hang around positive people. Negative people have that sour look and are a real downer to be around. So put on that pleasant face and keep those negative, sarcastic comments to yourself.

💣* *Being too intense or serious all the time.* Sometimes we need to be serious. But ALL the time is a drag – for you and others around you. Everyone needs

to have fun once in awhile. So, look for something you enjoy, and get out there and do it.

💣 *Bragging.* If you are really good at something, you don't need to tell others. They will see it by your actions.

💣 *Moaning or whining all the time.* This gets old really fast. Whining is hard on the ears and sends people running faster than almost anything.

💣 *Being a bully.* This is another one where you need to think about the Golden Rule. If you don't want someone to tease you, don't tease them. If you don't want someone to be mean to you, don't be mean to others.

💣 *Claiming credit for something you didn't do.* Be proud of what you do. Let others be proud of what they do.

💣* Lying or cheating. This is a matter of trust. Friends like to trust their friends. If you lie or cheat, it is difficult to trust you.

Kids Are Picking on Me . . .

What Should I Do?

You are probably asking yourself: *Am I being bullied? This sure feels AWFUL.*

Is this a bad day or what?

"Bullied" is a strong word. I don't know.

Bullying is kind of like fighting. It is play fighting when two friends are messing around and wrestling. It may look like fighting, but because both are enjoying it, they are actually playing. If one or both are not enjoying it, then it is fighting. Teasing is the same way. If both people are having fun and just kidding each other, then there is no problem. But, unless it is a two-way-street and BOTH are having fun, then it is definitely bullying. So, if you don't like what is being done to you, IT IS BULLYING and they need to stop it.

The Test. *(Don't panic! You don't have to study for this one. Just look over the list.)* You are being bullied if these things are happening to you AND you don't like it.

- Calling you names that hurt your feelings
- Writing unkind things about you and putting them where others can read them – *like the bathroom walls*
- Making things up to try to get you into trouble
- Hitting, pinching, biting, pushing and shoving or any other act of aggression
- Threatening to beat you up
- Taking things away from you
- Damaging or breaking your belongings
- Stealing money or things from you
- Taking your friends away from you
- Spreading rumors about you or your family whether it is true or not

- Threatening and intimidating you
- Making phone calls where they say things that hurt your feelings – sometimes they don't talk at all
- Embarrassing you in front of others by calling you names or doing something to you, like pulling your seat out from under you, or hiding your pencil or book, for instance
- Telling other kids not to talk to you or to be friends with you (*Really hitting below the belt*)
- "Accidentally" falling into you or shoving you in the hall *(Accident? Riiiight)*
- Sexually harassing you like following you around, whistling at you when you walk by, or making comments about your body

You might be so hurt or scared or unhappy that you don't want to go to school. You might even pretend to be sick. It is all right to feel that way – you probably DO feel sick. Being bullied can feel awful. But no matter how bad it makes you feel, you are not alone.

And, even though you might feel helpless sometimes, there are some things you can do to help yourself. The main thing you have to remember though is this: IT IS NOT YOUR FAULT YOU ARE BEING BULLIED. NO ONE DESERVES TO BE BULLIED.

Sometimes, others don't know that they are making you feel bad – they think they are just teasing and you are having as much fun as they are. Sometimes, they are being just plain mean.

If the bullying has just begun, you might be able to get it stopped on your own. You might want to try to solve the problem on your own if someone is talking to you in a rude tone of voice or is being openly unfriendly – like refusing to be near you or sit near you – or calling you names or saying hurtful things to you. If they are not doing these things in front of others to embarrass you, you might be able to get it stopped before things get ugly. Tell the person that you don't like what they are doing, and that you would like them to stop. Let's hope that does it. If not and the person continues to taunt you, they are intending to bully you. It must stop. There are things that you can do to stop the bully. You deserve nothing less.

If you are being bullied, follow these steps.

1. Give them the Stone Face.
First off, just what is a stone face? You keep your face totally expressionless – show absolutely no emotion. It is a kind of a "deer in the headlights" look – like your face is made of stone. This keeps you from reacting

and showing any emotion to what they are saying.

Kids tease and bully because they want to SEE a reaction. It's like pushing a button. *"Hey Bob, look. If I go up to So-and-so and tell him he's a loser, he will cry. It works every time."* If you don't give the bully what he wants – YOUR REACTION – he will probably quit. You might have to keep it up for awhile, but eventually they will get bored and decide to leave you alone.

I don't know if I can do it. What they say DOES get to me. How do I keep that stone face when I just want to cry and run away? Here is a trick: IN YOUR MIND tell yourself over and over "I will not let you get me upset. I am strong! I am confident! I am a better person than you! I will not let you get me upset. I am strong! I am confident! I am a better person than you! I will not let you get me upset . . ."

2. Tell them to stop it

You wouldn't think you would have to do this, but sometimes others are clueless. They might not know that what they have said is bothering you. If this is the case, then this will stop the teasing right away. But, alas, some kids are just not nice and asking them to stop in a nice way will not work. For these kids, tell them FIRMLY to stop it! You may even have to shout it. (Buzz off! or No! or Go Away!) Say it angrily – with that stone face, remember. Then turn and walk away. Make it hard for the bully. Make it very obvious that you don't like what they are doing, and you won't stand there and listen. Hint: Practice your No! and Go Away! in the mirror until you have it just the way you want it.

Sometimes it is a group of kids bothering you. Yep, that's the way some bullies are. Too scared to do the deed by themselves, they gang up on someone. If this happens to you, look the weakest person in the group right in the eye, put on your best stone face, and say something like "I don't think this is very funny, do you?" *By now you should have that stone face look down to a fine science.* Then walk away.

3. Keep walking.

If you can, keep walking. Make the person making your life miserable make a spectacle of himself by following you. If you are in a place with other people, walk near some of those people. This is a lot like the stone face but you are walking at the same time. Just keep walking where you are going repeating IN YOUR MIND "I will not let you get me upset. I am strong! I am confident! I am a better person than you! I will not let you get me upset. I am strong! I am confident! I am a better person than you! I will not let you get me upset . . ."

While you are walking with that stone face, you might want to be planning where to go. Ask yourself: Where is the best place to go when I am being bullied? Where would a bully not follow me?

4. Go to a safe place.
Find witnesses. There is safety in numbers; bullies don't like witnesses. Stay in areas where there are plenty of other people. Besides, you might need someone to back up your story. If possible, stand by a friend or an adult. *Teachers work really great for this one.*

On the school bus, ask to sit near the driver. If she asks why, tell her. She can keep an eye out for possible problems. If it is an ordinary bus, sit by other adults. (Bullies don't want witnesses – especially adults.) It wouldn't even hurt to tell the adult why you want to sit next to them. They have kids; they will understand.

5. Report it to an adult.

You might think you can handle this on your own or that the bully will stop if you don't tell anyone. The truth is, the bully probably will not stop until you report it. So, tell your parents, tell the school counselor, tell a teacher, tell a policeman – any adult you feel you can talk to. If you tell an adult, and he or she has not been able to stop the bullying, tell another adult. If you are afraid to go alone, take someone with you. This may be hard to talk about and having someone with you will make it less scary.

I don't think I can face anyone right now. Telling someone in person is better, but if you really can't do that, write a note telling what is happening and how you feel.

But this is so embarrassing – admitting that someone is picking on me, and I can't make them stop. Everyone needs help sometime. This just happens to be your time. It doesn't make you weak to ask for help. Actually, you are a strong person to ask for help. It takes guts to tell someone what is going on, and that you need help. Take a deep breath. Now, go tell someone what is happening.

I don't know. I've always been told not to tattle. Isn't this tattling? NO. Tattling is when you tell on someone just to get them into trouble. In this case you aren't telling "just" to get them into trouble. You are reporting something that will keep you (or someone else if you see someone else being bullied) safe from attack and harassment. You should not be silent when you or someone else is being tormented and hurt. Everyone has the right to be safe from attacks and harassment.

Actually, I'm not embarrassed. I'm afraid that if I tell someone I'm being bullied and get the bully in trouble, things will get worse. I just want it to go away. It is all right to be afraid. The bully is making your life miserable. But, if you don't report this, the bullying will most likely continue – and probably get worse. Also, there is a good chance that the adults can put a stop to the bullying without the bully knowing that you told. The bully may be harassing more than one person – he won't know which one told. The adults can watch the bully closely so that he can be caught red-handed. But even if the bully does find out that you told, it is better to have things out in the open. And it will send a message to this bully and others that you will not take being harassed and they will be in trouble if they bother you.

Bullies will not stop unless they are reported. If you see anyone else being bullied (even your worst enemy), tell an adult about it.

I'm not the one being bullied. But there is another kid whose life must be miserable. I'm afraid if I tell someone about what the bully is doing, he will start picking on me. I wouldn't wish that on my worst enemy. No one has to know that you reported the bullying. You can make up an excuse to stay after class: you didn't understand the assignment or you forgot when a paper was due. Wait until everyone else is gone. That way you can tell the teacher without anyone else overhearing. Or you can stop into the counselor's office between classes and tell him what is gong on. They will keep your secret. People who are being bullied need friends. If you can help someone from being harassed or attacked, you should do it.

IF YOU ARE UNSURE WHETHER OR NOT TO MAKE A REPORT, PLEASE MAKE ONE! It is better to be safe than sorry.

Things have gotten better. But there is not always going to be an adult around to help. It will probably happen again sometime. Isn't there something I can do if someone starts teasing and harassing me? Sure. Maybe we can get this teasing and harassing stopped in its tracks. Look these over and pick one or two that you think might work for you.

☞ Say "So!"

If someone makes a nasty remark about you, your comeback can be "so" or "yeah, whatever". Then walk off. This keeps you from reacting in a way that the bully will want. It will also show them that what they said is not having an effect on you. They are left standing there with their mouth open – and speechless. They will be less likely to make hurtful comments to you another time.

☞ Ask the bully to repeat what they said.

Pretend that you did not hear what they said. With that stone face, ask the bully to repeat the remark. This is definitely not the reaction the bully wanted, and not something they had planned on. This will actually give you some control over the situation.

☞ Tell a friend what is happening.

Friends are like instant witnesses. It will be harder for the bully to pick on you if you always have someone with you. So, the trick here is to travel in pairs or groups.

☞ Try to stand up to the person who is bullying you.

Bullies try to pick on people they think will take it. If they think you will stand there and take it, they will keep picking on you. Tell the person to stop. Then, if they don't, report it to an adult.

☞ **Think of a few snappy comebacks and have them ready.**

Kids who bully others pick on those who are easily upset. Their prize is the emotional reaction they get when they tease and harass. If you can have a snappy comeback ready, you will be ahead of the game. Practice saying them in front of the mirror at home. Then, when the bully comes up to you and begins to tease, give him your snappy comeback. Who knows, the bully might decide that you are not who he wants to pick on. If you need help with snappy comebacks, there is a list in the back of the book of some that other kids have used.

I'm beginning to get the hang of this now, and it is better. Are there some things that would keep me from being picked on at all?

☞ **Pay attention to your BODY LANGUAGE.**

Bullies have been known to pick their victims by looking at body language. When you walk into school, do you feel shy, worried, and sad? Or do you feel powerful, confident, and happy?

People who feel powerful, confident, and happy walk with their chin up and eyes forward. They look where they are going and walk purposefully to get there. A bully will usually stay clear. Bullies want someone who will crumble at their taunting remarks.

People who feel shy, worried, or sad, on the other hand, many times walk looking at the ground. They tend to take small steps and sometimes shuffle their feet. They try not to draw attention to themselves. They look like they are on the defensive and want to be left alone. These are the people that bullies have a tendency to pick on. *"Look Martha. She looks like she's having a bad day. Let's make it worse."* It's a little like stamping on your forehead: "I am a victim."

Look around. Find someone that looks confident. Study him or her carefully paying close attention to body language. At home, practice walking this way. Practice until it feels comfortable and natural to walk in this more confident way.

So, even if you do feel shy, worried, sad, or lonely, make a real effort not to wear your feelings like your clothes.
☺ Step out boldly with confidence
☺ Look where you are going with your chin up
☺ Put a pleasant expression on your face
This will send a message to bullies that you are not an easy target. You may not be very confident on the inside, but those around you only see what is on the outside. Now, your outside self looks confident and in control.

☞ **Stay where there are people.**
Kids who tease and harass others like to pick on those who are by themselves. It makes the bully's job easier, and they are most likely to

get away with it. So, do yourself a favor and hang out where other people are.

☞ Don't be alone in places where you think the bully might pick on you.

First of all, you might want to avoid some places altogether. You could change your route to and from school or leave at different times each day. It is also a good idea not to follow a routine. That way the bully can't find a pattern in what you are doing and ambush you. If you make it too hard for the bully to pick on you, he may move on. Be creative. The harder you make it for the bully, the less likely he will mess with you.

☞ Talk to others who are being teased and harassed.

It is easy to crawl into a shell when you are being bullied; you may feel lonely and without friends. But you are not the only one spending your lunch and class breaks hiding and staying to yourself. Look around. If you see someone else walking or standing alone, try to start a conversation: about the English assignment, about the game this week, about anything. This might not work the first time, but sooner or later you will find someone who will want to be a friend and that you can talk to about what is happening to both of you.

☞ Keep a diary.

When something happens, write down the date, details, and your feelings. First, it always helps to get something off your chest. *Whew.* You will also have the date and details of what has been happening when you report it to an adult.

☞ **Sign up for a self-defense course.**
This will give you more confidence and will naturally help with body language. As you feel more confident, you will naturally walk with more confidence. Don't confuse this with learning to fight, though. You never want to start a fight. But you will have more confidence that if you ARE attacked, you will be able to defend yourself.

☹ **THINGS THAT WON'T WORK**

☞ **Ignoring the situation.**
This is different than the stone face. The stone face helps you not react and give the bully what he wants. But even though you give the stone face, you must report it if the person doesn't stop when you ask them to. Ignoring it sends the message to the bully that you will take it, and he might continue to give it.

☞ **Trying to handle it on your own.**
Some things we can handle on our own, but this isn't one of them. If you have asked the bully to stop and they are still making your life miserable, get some help.

☞ **Fighting back.**
Most bullies are bigger and stronger than you are – that is why they are picking on you. If you fight back, you will most likely make

everything worse. Even worse, you might be blamed for starting the fight. Bullies are sneaky like foxes. They have a knack for picking on you, and then making it look like you are the one who is causing trouble. Take my advice. Report it to an adult – immediately! Then, there will be no mistake as to who started the trouble.

☺ WHY, WHY, WHY DO SOME KIDS PICK ON OTHERS?

The why's are many. Some kids pick on others all the time. They seem to get a kick out of it. Some kids do it only every once in awhile. Sometimes, kids begin to pick on others because they have been victims in the past. Do any of these sound familiar?

- Other kids are doing it
- I want to hang out with the cool crowd and this is what they do
- I'm getting tired of getting picked on. If I hang out with this crowd, I won't get picked on
- It's the best way to keep others from bullying me. If people think of me as a bully, then no one will pick on me
- It makes me feel better than the person I'm bullying
- It makes me feel stronger than the person I'm bullying
- It makes me feel smarter than they are, too

I'm Always in Trouble . . .

What Should I Do?

☺ THINGS THAT WORK

Think, think, think, think, think before you act. You have a conscience that is sitting on your shoulder saying no, no, no, no, NO. But, the trouble is, you haven't been listening to your conscience. Before you do anything that is at all questionable, STOP. Take a DEEEEEEP breath. Then ask your conscience: "Should I be doing this?" If your conscience isn't being much help today with answers, ask

yourself some questions. First, are there any negative consequences to this action? If there are, stop now. Back up and walk away. This is something you should NOT be doing. Get out of there as fast as you can. Second, if you are unsure about negative consequences, then ask yourself, are there any positive consequences to this action? If the answer here is yes (and you really can think of no negative consequences), then proceed. You might want to proceed *with caution,* but you may proceed.

☞ **Think, think, think, think, think before you react.**

There that conscience is again, sitting on your shoulder. This time the conscience is shouting no, no, no, NO, NO!!! Always before, you reacted and didn't listen to your conscience. You have a great conscience that is trying to help you, but you have to give it time. When something happens – like someone bumps you, or even worse hits you or takes something from you that is yours or whatever -- if you react, probably your action is going to be one that will get you into trouble. First, STOP. TAKE A DEEEEP BREATH. If it is something you can handle immediately in a calm manner, you can try to talk it out right then. If it is something that just has *"this is going to get out of hand"* *written all over it,* step back and get out of there. It is better to walk away. If something needs to be done, you can always go back later and do whatever needs to be done. But at least this time, you will have thought out what the best way to act is and have let your conscience do its job. This time you can act in such a way that there are positive consequences rather than negative. One thing I have learned in life is *"There are consequences for everything we do. The trick is to do the things that will have **positive** consequences for us."*

☞ **Ask others why they think you are always in trouble.**

Sometimes, it has been so long that we have felt those positive consequences that our conscience is just not much help. Your conscience might need some help to get back on track. Everyone has a conscience; you could ask to borrow someone else's conscience for awhile. Find someone who will give you an honest answer. Ouch! The answers sometimes hurt – but not as much as always being in trouble.

☹ THINGS THAT WON'T WORK

☞ **Blaming others.**

Nice try, but it isn't going to work. If you have been in trouble a lot, people are on to you anyway. And worse, even when you don't do it, you are sometimes going to be blamed for it just because you have the reputation of being in trouble. So, if you do fall back into old habits and act or react poorly and get into trouble, admit it. At least people will respect you for being honest.

☞ **Not accepting responsibility for your actions.**

This goes along with blaming others. I know you are going to try to think before you do things and act and react in positive ways. But, you are not perfect. Everything takes time to fix. When you fall back into old habits, at least take responsibility for what you did. That way, others can see that you are trying to improve by being at least willing to admit that you were wrong and will accept the consequences for your actions.

My Teacher Doesn't Like Me . . .

What Should I Do?

Yeah, yeah, yeah, I know. You have been picked on since the very first day. The first day of school, the teacher watches as all the students walk in the door. *"Yes, Yes, Yes,"* she says with a smile. *"Oh, no! That one's hair is messed up. I don't like that one."* She continues, *"Yes, Yes. Oh! There's another one. Look at that silly grin – he has trouble written all over him. I don't like that one either."*

Okay, I'm being really sarcastic here. You know that your teacher doesn't really do this. So, if she doesn't like you, there has to be something that you are doing – like talking when you are not supposed to, showing off for others and distracting them, rolling your eyes at her, and things like that. If you are doing things that are annoying your teacher, you are not making her day a pleasant one. She really may not enjoy seeing you. Come on now, you're making her life miserable, right. Would you enjoy being around someone who does that to you? And now, to make matters worse, you may have a reputation for poor behavior. So, if she is helping another student and hears something behind her, she may assume it is you causing the problem when it may not be. You will get away with nothing. Your reputation will now begin to get you in trouble, and your next complaint will probably be that your teacher picks on you. She is not picking on you intentionally, but when there is a disruption, she will probably assume it is you if she doesn't see it happen. So, what do you?

☺ THINGS THAT WORK

☞ **Tell her you're sorry.** Take responsibility for your poor behavior. Tell your teacher you are going to try to do better. That should get things going in the right direction. Your teacher will appreciate your wanting to improve and will see you in a better light.

☞ **Be on your best behavior.**

 Be the perfect student. The bottom line: Treat your teacher like you would want to be treated if you were in her shoes. The old saying *"don't criticize someone else until you have walked a mile in his or her shoes"* really

does make sense. She has a very tough job. Treat her like you would want to be treated if you were up there in front of the class:

☼ When the teacher is talking, be sure that you are paying attention.

☼ The class doesn't need a clown. It may get boring sometimes, but the worst thing you can do is to entertain the class. Actually, that is the teacher's job. She has things she wants the class to learn and, hopefully, a somewhat entertaining way to do that. If you entertain, you are getting in her way big time.

☞ **Like her and she will like you back.**
If you treat your teacher nicely, she will begin to treat you better also. You still must improve your behavior (and your reputation), but if you begin to act better in class AND treat her nicely (a smile and "good morning" really helps), she will stop assuming you are the culprit whenever something goes wrong. She may even begin to like you.

☞ **Be respectful to your teacher.**
No rolling the eyes, making tacky remarks, saying things under your breath, laughing at her, mimicking her, or anything else like that. The two of you may have a generation gap thing going on, and you may not really like her. But she is doing her best to help you be the best you can be, so at least give her credit for that.

☹ THINGS THAT WON'T WORK

☞ **Complaining.**
Whining and complaining will get you no where. Whining to your teacher will only annoy her more. Whining and complaining to your parents will only annoy them, and even if you get them to call the teacher and complain that you are being treated unfairly, this is not going to help your reputation with her. (If you think she dislikes you now, do you think she is going to like you any better after your parents chew on her – NO WAY!) You have to take responsibility for your part in this and improve your behavior before anything will improve at school.

☞ **Rolling your eyes.**
Definitely not going to help. Even a little eye roll is a no-no. If your teacher calls you down, just say *"okay."* A little *"I'm sorry; "I'll try to do better"* wouldn't hurt your situation any either.

☞ **Mumbling under your breath or talking back.**
For sure don't go there – hugely disrespectful – much worse than the eye roll. The teacher may think you said something you didn't, and this could get you in real trouble. And talking back may even land you in the principal's office – a place you definitely don't want to be. You might as well start humming the song *"Bad Boys, Bad Boys. Whatcha goina do? Whatcha goina do when they come for you?"*

Excuses

☺ THOSE THAT WORK

☞ **Nothing!!!!** This may seem harsh because there really are some very good reasons why you haven't done what was asked of you. So, although some excuses are valid and real, an excuse is never the answer. The bottom line is that you have to do what needs to be done, no matter how many problems you have getting there. When an excuse slaps you down, get up, dust yourself off, fix it, and get yourself going again. Besides, teachers have heard just about everything. It would be really hard to think of something that your teacher hasn't already heard a million times before. There are some very original excuses used over the years and, yes, some of the same ones are used over and over. They didn't work when your grandma was in school, and unfortunately, they won't work now. There are some new high-tech excuses. Too bad, sometimes there really is a good reason why you didn't get your homework done. Many times, though, the real problem here is a big word called **p r o c r a s t i n a t i o n**. If you had started earlier on the assignment, then when that PROBLEM came up, you would have had time to fix it.

☹ THOSE THAT WON'T WORK.

☞ **My dog ate my homework**.
Not very original, but it happens sometimes. It happened to me on a college paper. I got a new puppy, and he proceeded to chew up my assignment. I was too embarrassed to even tell the instructor what had happened. I just sucked it up and took the consequences.

☞ *It's in my mom's car.*
Probably true. But it isn't in the teacher's hands, and it is such an often-used excuse that your teacher probably won't believe you anyway.

☞ *The computer crashed/ the printer is out of ink and so on and on.*
With technology, this does happen and is a good excuse. The only trouble is that you have just admitted to the teacher that you are, oh, so guilty of p r o c r a s t i n a t i o n. Give yourself a couple of days before the assignment is due to type it. That way, if the computer or printer goes belly-up, you have time to punt and do something different. (You could always go back to the dark ages and write – neatly, of course – the assignment if worse came to worse.)

☞ *My little sister used it for a coloring book*.
It happens. But, hey, your paper is colorful and at least the teacher knows you did it. If you have time, you could do the paper over. If

not, hand it in the way it is. Your teacher probably won't mind the extra color or artwork anyway.

☞ *It's at home; I forgot it.*
Your paper might actually be at home. But this is the most used excuse of all time. What this really means to a teacher is "I don't have it done and need an extra day to work on it." This one definitely won't work.

It's in my locker somewhere; I know it is.
Just give me a few minutes to look.

Appendix 1

I know that avoiding bullies is one of your top priorities. But, there are going to be times when you run into someone who can't resist the urge to have some fun at your expense. Here are some comebacks that have worked. They might catch the bully off guard. They are definitely not the reaction the bully expected. Pick a few that you think will work for you and try them out.

What to Say to a Bully

- Whatever!
- Yeah, right.
- Thank you.
- Get a life.
- Are you done yet?
- Are you finished yet?
- Do you have anything new to say?
- Whatever you say. You're the expert.
- Well, you're sure a mean person.
- Yeah, yeah. What else is new.
- Do you feel better now?
- Stop wasting your time -- and mine.
- You really got me with that one. You can stop now.

- Do we have to keep doing the same thing over and over?
- I'm impressed. You're an expert – at being mean.
- What did you say? Are you talking to me?
- You must feel pretty lousy all the time to treat people the way you do.
- You've made your point. Happy now?
- Are we going to do this again? Whatever.
- You've apparently never heard of the Golden Rule.
- Would you like it if someone were doing this to you?
- Would you like it if someone were doing this to your brother (sister)?
- Surely you have something better to do.
- Are you getting tired of this yet?
- Would you just stop?
- Hurry up and finish with this nonsense so we can both get on our way.
- You again? You're really becoming annoying.
- That's really funny.
- I heard you, but I don't really care.
- Are you satisfied now?
- How can you say mean things like that with a smile on your face?
- Why don't you just grow up!
- Act your age why don't you.
- Well, that's immature.

- I could care less.
- You know, you're using me to feel good about yourself is really getting old.
- You used to be pretty cool.
- Boy, have you changed!
- I never thought you would turn out this way.
- I never thought you could do something as mean as this.
- I thought you were a nice person until now.
- I thought you were pretty cool, but I guess I was wrong.
- And to think we used to be friends.
- I'm disappointed. I thought we could have been friends.
- You're hooked. You can't stop doing this can you?
- Say whatever you want. You're not going to get to me.
- Go ahead. Keep talking. I'm not listening.
- Well, aren't you the king of put downs.
- Are you bored yet? I know I am.
- Go bother somebody else.
- Do I look like someone who cares?
- Go bother someone who cares what you have to say.
- You can leave me alone now.
- Ha . . . . Ha . . . . Ha.
- You're wrong if you think this is going to make you popular.

- You should hear what people are saying about you behind your back.
- I'll admit it. You're better than me. So you can stop now.
- I'd hate to be you.
- It would suck to be you.
- What did I ever do to you to deserve this?
- I know I should feel bad about this, but you're not worth it.
- Is this the only way you can build your self esteem?
- OK, I'm hurt. Now move on to your next victim.
- Those are only words. Here are some new words: Who cares?
- I feel sorry for you.
- Is this your only goal in life?
- What a waste.
- Are we going to do this every day?
- Don't you have anything else? I heard that one in first grade.
- If you don't stop this, I will report it.
- My little brother (sister) does a better job of making me feel bad than you.
- Is that all you've got?
- That's it?
- Well, I'm impressed. You have discovered that I look different than you.

- Well, I'm impressed. You have discovered that I am different than you.
- Everyone has a talent. Is this YOUR only one?
- So . . . . that is supposed to make me feel what?
- What were you saying? I wasn't listening.
- Congratulations! You are the best at this.
- Doesn't it bother you that this is what you're known for? Nice reputation.
- I should probably report this, but you're not worth the effort.
- Do you really think you upset me? Think again.

The 10 School

I.
Thou shalt follow the Golden Rule.
Treat others as you would like to be
treated.

II.
Thou shalt be prepared for class every
day. Bring needed books and supplies.

III.
Thou shalt turn in assignments
completely finished and on time.

IV.
Remember thy school day and be
there every day – on time.

V.
Honor thy teacher and thy principal.

Commandments

VI.
Thou shalt not give dirty looks that could kill.

VII.
Thou shalt have pride in yourself and your school.

VIII.
Be yourself. You are a unique person. Let others see the real you.

IX.
Thou shalt not say untrue or mean things about others.

X.
Thou shalt not covet thy neighbor's work. Do your own.

Order Form

Postal orders: English *and Math* Through...
c/o Merry L. Gumm
1482 51st Road
Douglass, KS 67039
Website orders: englishthrough.com
Email orders: order@englishthrough.com

Please send the following books and kits:

Item	Price
_____	$ _____
_____	_____
_____	_____

Shipping and Handling: $ 1.75

Sales Tax: KS residents add 6.75%   _____

     Total Due $_____

Name_____

Address_____
           City   State   Zip

Email address or telephone _____

Payment: ☐ Check: Enclosed with order
☐ Credit Card:
Card Number _____

Last 3 digits on the back of card _____

Name on card _____

Expiration date: _____

English and Math Through...
A Child's World

Where learning is fun!

Visit our website:
englishthrough.com